ANNE FRANK

Voice of Hope

Kristen Woronoff

BLACKBIRCH PRESS

THOMSON
™
GALE

Detroit • New York • San Diego • San Francisco
Boston • New Haven, Conn. • Waterville, Maine
London • Munich

Published by Blackbirch Press
10911 Technology Place
San Diego, CA 92127
e-mail: customerservice@galegroup.com
Web site: http://www.galegroup.com/blackbirch

© 2002 Blackbirch Press
an imprint of the Gale Group

Printed in China

10 9 8 7 6 5 4 3 2 1

Photo credits:
Cover, pages 3, 7, 9, 13 © Hulton Archive/Getty Images; page 4, 6, 22-23, 24-25, 30 © AP/Wide World Photos; page 5 © Richard Freimark, courtesy of USHMM Photo Archives; page 8, 20, 21, 26, 29 © CORBIS; page 9, 10, 11, 12, 13, 14, 27 © Anne Frank Stichting, Amsterdam; page 16 © Nederlands Instituut voor Oorlogsdocumentatie, courtesy of USHMM Photo Archives; page 17 © USHMM Photo Archives; page 20 © Bundesarchiv, courtesy of USHMM Photo Archives; page 28 © Photofest

Library of Congress Cataloging-in-Publication Data
Woronoff, Kristen.
Anne Frank / by Kristen Woronoff.
        p. cm. — (Famous women juniors)
Summary: Introduces the life of the teenage girl who dreamed of becoming a writer someday, but who died in a Nazi death camp without seeing her diary become famous around the world.
        ISBN 1-56711-586-1 (Hardcover : alk. paper)
1. Frank, Anne, 1929-1945—Juvenile literature. 2. Jewish children in the Holocaust—Netherlands—Amsterdam—Biography—Juvenile literature. 3.
Jews—Netherlands—Amsterdam—Biography—Juvenile literature. 4. Holocaust, Jewish (1939-1945)—Netherlands—Amsterdam—Biography—Juvenile literature. 5.
Amsterdam (Netherlands)—Biography—Juvenile literature. [1. Frank, Anne, 1929-1945. 2. Jews—Netherlands—Biography. 3. Holocaust, Jewish (1939-1945)—Netherlands—Amsterdam. 4. Women—Biography.] I. Title. II. Series.

DS135.N6 F7388 2002
940.53'18'092—dc21   2001005068

Anne Frank was a 13-year-old in the 1940s. That's why she started keeping a diary. Like many teenagers, Anne felt that her parents didn't understand her. She could not figure out the boys she knew. And she did not like some of her teachers.

Anne didn't think she was a good writer. One of her teachers said her stories were average.

But today, millions of people have read Anne's diary. Anne Frank's name is known around the world. The place where she wrote her famous diary is now a museum.

Anne wrote during World War II. It was one of the most terrible times in history. Anne died in the "Holocaust," a word that means "great fire." The Holocaust happened in Europe. More than 6 million Jews were murdered in the Holocaust.

Anne Frank was born in Germany. When she was born, a group called the Nazis was taking control of the country. Nazis hated all Jews. Anne and her family were Jewish.

Synagogues were destroyed throughout Europe during the Holocaust.

Before the War

The Frank family lived in Frankfurt, Germany. Anne's father, Otto Frank, worked in department stores. He had once been a soldier in the German army. In 1925, Otto married Edith Hollander. Their first daughter, Margot, was born the next year. Anne was born in 1929.

When Anne was born, the Great Depression was spreading around the world. Stores closed and people lost their jobs. Many people, especially people in Germany, were worried about the future. The Nazi leader, Adolf Hitler, promised Germans a better life.

Adolf Hitler was the leader of the Nazis.

Hitler blamed Jews for everything that was wrong in Germany. Get rid of these "outsiders," he said, and Germany's problems would end. Soon, Hitler and his Nazi Party ruled Germany.

With Nazis in power, Jews in Germany were mistreated. Many had to close their stores and quit their jobs. They had to follow strict rules. People who complained were sent to special prisons. These prisons were called concentration camps.

Jewish shops and businesses were destroyed during the Holocaust.

Anne was thin with dark brown hair, dark eyes, and dimples in her cheeks. Her sister, Margot, got better grades in school. She was also neat and well behaved. Anne was messier. Her strong personality sometimes got her into trouble at school.

Margot was quiet. Anne, however, often got attention by making people laugh. When she was four years old, her mother called her "a little clown."

By 1935, Jews in Germany had lost all of their rights. In 1938, all Jewish students were banned from German schools.

Then the Nazis began arresting Jews. About 30,000 Jews were sent to concentration camps. All German Jews were forced to wear a yellow star to show that they were "different." Many Jews left Germany and moved to other countries to be safe.

Anne's father, Otto, decided to get his family out of Germany. He found a job in Amsterdam, Holland. He thought Holland would be a safe place. He brought his family there. But he was wrong—Holland was not safe at all.

Jews were forced to wear yellow stars in public.

On May 10, 1940, the Franks heard that the German army had attacked Holland. They knew the Nazis would make Holland just like Germany. Anne and all other Jews under Nazi rule had to wear yellow stars. They had to follow strict rules.

Soon, all-out war had begun. World War II was becoming the deadliest war in history.

On June 12, 1942, Anne turned 13 years old. Her father's present to her was a diary—a book with blank pages and a hard, checkered cover. In it, Anne could write about what happened each day. She named the book "Kitty." Anne could tell Kitty anything.

Anne's family hid in an attic in this building to avoid the Nazis.

Into Hiding

By this time, many Jews were hiding from Nazis. They hid in attics, basements, or extra rooms. In the summer of 1942, Anne's parents found a hiding place. It was the storage space above the office where Mr. Frank worked. He called it the "Annex."

Anne's father told one woman he worked with about the plan. Her name was Miep Gies. She promised to keep the family's hiding place a secret. She also promised to bring them food and anything else they needed until the war ended.

Anne and her family did not hide in the Annex alone. Another Jewish man, Mr. Van Daan, his wife, and his son, Peter, hid there too.

Miep Gies helped the Franks survive in the Annex.

Anne had little time to pack for the Annex. The first thing she packed was her diary, Kitty. Anne could not say goodbye to her friends because her family's secret might have gotten out.

"I'm very afraid that we shall be discovered and be shot," Anne wrote in one of her first diary entries. She also wrote about daily life in the Annex.

The entrance to the Annex was hidden by a bookcase.

At Mr. Frank's office, a bookcase covered the entrance to the hiding space. The bookcase swung out like a door.

The space had two small rooms on the second floor. It also had a large room on the third floor. At night, this large room was Mr. and Mrs. Van Daan's bedroom. Peter, and his cat, Mouschi, slept on the floor. There was also an attic. Anne liked to go there to read.

Soon, another Jew moved into the Annex. His name was Dr. Albert Dussel. He was a dentist.

During the day, people in the Annex walked around in stocking feet so workers downstairs would not hear them. They waited until evening to flush the toilet because it would make too much noise.

Anne felt close to her father. But she and her mother did not always get along. Sometimes the Van Daans and Dr. Dussel bothered her, too.

Workers arrived downstairs at 8:30 A.M. and stayed until 5:30 P.M. For those hours, there had to be total silence in the Annex. Miep Gies brought up food and supplies after the workers left.

Otto Frank

Edith Frank

Dr. Dussel joined the families in the Annex.

Anne went to bed at 10 P.M. and got up at 7 A.M. Sometimes, however, the roar of German guns woke her at night.

During the day, Anne read and studied. And, most days, she wrote in her diary. Anne liked to write when she was alone. Sometimes the others teased her about her "secret" writing.

The dining room and living room of the Annex.

A model of the entire Annex.

After a year, living conditions in the Annex became worse. The eight people had only bread for breakfast. They suffered stomachaches. Clothes began to wear out. The sleeves of Anne's sweaters reached only halfway down her arms. To make things worse, Mouschi, Peter's cat, had fleas.

Anne had terrible headaches. But it was too dangerous for her to go to the doctor.

By 1942, Jews in Germany, Austria, Poland and other places were being rounded up.

Outside the Annex, Nazis continued to punish and kill Jews. "Children coming home from school find that their parents have disappeared," Anne wrote in her diary. Anne felt guilty that her family was surviving while other Jews suffered. Soon conditions for all Jews would become even worse.

In 1942, the Nazis decided to solve their Jewish "problem" by sending Jews to death camps. There, Jews were either worked to death or killed.

Anne tried to feel hopeful. But it was hard to believe things would get better. Everyone in the Annex had become pale. In December 1943, Anne came down with the flu.

Anne found it hard to get along with the others. But she always reminded herself how much worse her life could be.

To lighten their mood, Anne and her father wrote funny poems to each other. They also made presents from whatever was lying around. Miep once gave Anne's spirits a boost when she brought her a pair of high-heeled shoes.

At concentration camps, Jews were treated as prisoners and eventually killed.

Inset: Inmates at a concentration camp

By 1944, Anne was almost 15 years old. She had lived in the Annex for a year and a half.

As Anne grew up, she began to have feelings for Peter Van Daan, who was 17. Sometimes they talked for hours. After a while, however, Anne's feelings for Peter cooled. They became just good friends.

On June 6, 1944, American, British, and other forces landed in France to fight the Germans. The Franks thought this meant the Germans would be forced to leave Amsterdam. Then they could come out of hiding.

On June 6, 1944—D-Day—U.S. forces landed on a beach in Normandy, France and began fighting in Europe.

This called for a celebration. A salesman had brought strawberries—a rare treat—for the workers downstairs. Miep took some upstairs and they were able to make jam.

The eight people in hiding were hopeful but still careful. They were always afraid they would be found. In 1943, the building was sold. The new owner might have found them, but a worker told the new landlord that he lost the key to the Annex. The new owner never asked about it again.

Anne and the others had good reason to be scared. The Nazis rewarded anyone who turned in Jews. They killed anyone who helped to hide Jews.

The Annex Is Discovered

On August 4, 1944, Miep was in the office downstairs. She looked up and saw a man pointing a gun at her. "Don't move," he said. Miep heard men entering other parts of the office. They seemed to know about the shelves that covered the secret entrance to the hiding place.

Nazi soldiers patrolled the streets, searching for Jews.

Otto Frank was giving Peter Van Daan an English lesson when he heard the footsteps. There was no time to run. The Dutch Nazi policemen rounded up the eight Jews. They had five minutes to pack. They all filled the little knapsacks they had kept ready for a quick escape.

Anne stored her diary in her father's briefcase. One of the policemen asked Otto Frank if he had any jewelry. Mr. Frank said he did not but that he had some silverware. The officer picked up the briefcase and emptied it so he could carry the silverware in it. Anne's diary fell out onto the floor.

Anne did not take her diary. The eight Jews were led downstairs at gunpoint. It was all done quietly. No one cried. They were put into a green police truck, which took them to the police station.

It was all over by noon. Later, Miep and another woman went upstairs. The Annex was empty, except for Mouschi, Peter's cat. They found Anne's diary on the floor and took it. Miep promised herself that she would keep it for Anne until she came back.

After the police station, the Franks, the Van Daans, and Dr. Dussel were taken to a Dutch prison called Westerbork. At Westerbork, the Franks remained together. Anne and Peter spent time together. They all hoped that the war would end soon. But those hopes ended in early September.

A young Polish boy surrenders to Nazis on the streets of Warsaw, Poland.

To the Death Camps

One day, the Nazis ordered the prisoners to prepare to move. That could only mean one thing: the death camps. The Franks and others at Westerbork were some of the last people sent to the camps.

Before leaving, parents made their children memorize the address of a place they would meet after the war. The Jews were put into freight cars. There were 75 people in each car. There was barely enough room to stand—with only one small window for fresh air.

After many days, the train stopped at Auschwitz, a death camp in Poland. When the doors opened, German guards stood outside with attack dogs. Women prisoners had to march for an hour to the camp called Birkenau. Children and old people were taken to gas chambers and killed.

Captured Jews are marched through downtown Warsaw, on their way to concentration camps.

24

Those who lived had little food and no warm clothes. Thousands froze to death or died from disease. Prisoners who became too weak to work were killed.

People who saw Anne at this time said she was still hopeful that the war would soon end. She, like other prisoners, had her head shaved and she wore a gray sack.

In October 1944, Anne and Margot were sent to a camp called Bergen-Belsen. Living conditions there were worse than in Birkenau.

Many people had typhus, a deadly disease that spreads quickly. Margot died from typhus first. Anne was also sick with the disease. In March 1945, Anne Frank died. She was 15 years old.

People were crowded together and starved at concentration camps.

Edith Frank died in the death camps in Poland. Dr. Dussel and Mr. and Mrs. Van Daan also died there. Peter was forced to march from Poland to Germany. The strain was too much, and he died.

Only Otto Frank stayed alive at Auschwitz. At the camp, he saw one of Anne's school friends. "Is Anne with you?" he asked. "Have you seen her or Margot?" The girl had not. Before the prisoners were freed, Otto learned that his wife had died.

After being freed, Anne's father went back to Amsterdam. He stayed with Miep Gies. Otto kept hoping that his daughters had survived. Six weeks after the war ended, he learned that they too had died.

Sharing the Diary

Part of Otto's sadness lifted when Miep shared Anne's diary with him. It was as though Anne's spirit was still alive.

The house where Anne and her family hid is now a museum.

Otto told friends about Anne's important writing. Many people said he should have it made into a book. At first he resisted, but then he gave in. He wanted the world to know about the horror of war through the eyes of a young girl.

Anne's diary was made into a play in 1955. The play was made into a movie in 1957. The Annex became a museum. Every year, many people visit the house to see where Anne Frank and seven other Jews hid from the Nazis.

The story of Anne and her diary was told in a play and then a movie, shown above.

Otto Frank at age 90

Over the years, many people have asked one question. Who told the Nazis about the Annex? Otto Frank did not wonder. "I don't want to know who did it," he said. Otto moved to Switzerland in 1952. In 1953, he married a woman who had also survived a concentration camp. He died in 1980. He was 90 years old.

Today, Anne's diary is still read by people around the world. Her lively and hopeful spirit lives on through her words. But those who read the diary also wonder what Anne would have been like as an adult. What might she have done? We will never know.

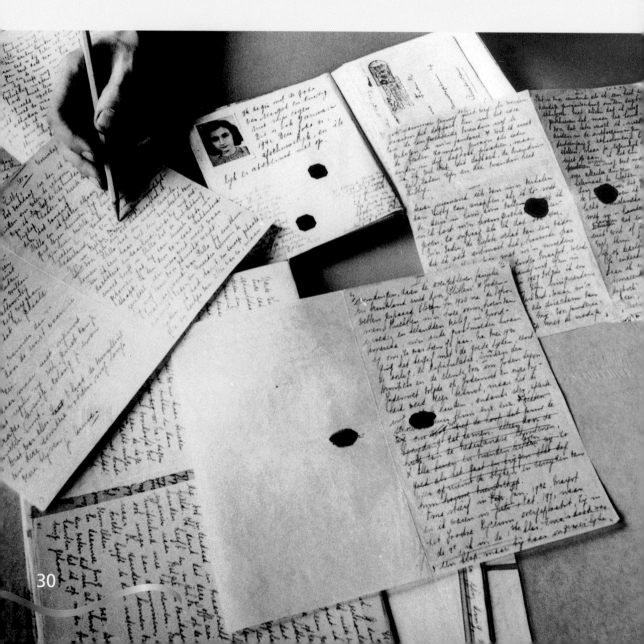

Glossary

Annex An added room.

Ban To forbid.

Concentration Camp A place where prisoners of war are detained.

Diary A personalized book used to write thoughts and feelings, or to record daily events.

Holocaust Great fire. The term is used to describe the mass murder of Jews by Nazis during World War II.

Typhus A severe disease marked by high fever, headaches, and rash.

For More Information

Website
Anne Frank Center, USA
www.annefrank.com

A comprehensive website that offers a biography of Anne, a bookstore, and a list of Anne Frank exhibits.

Books

Frank, Anne, edited by Otto Frank. *Anne Frank: The Diary of a Young Girl.* New York: Doubleday, 1995.

Gold, Alison Lee. *Memories of Anne Frank: Reflections of a Childhood Friend.* New York: Scholastic Paperbacks, 1999.

Hurwitz, Johanna. *Anne Frank: Life in Hiding.* New York: Camelot, 1999.

Pressler, Mirjam. *Anne Frank: A Hidden Life.* New York: Dutton Books, 2000.

Index

DATE			